# LUA Scripting Made Stupid Simple

### Authored By

### Jordan Kaufman

# DEDICATION

To my wife Jamie,
while(you.withMe == true) everyday++
*(sorry doesn't compile in Lua)*

# CONTENTS

# FREE GIFT – Lua Code in COLOR

## The Code Used in This Volume IN COLOR

Courtesy of our friend Derek Banas (from *New Think Tank*) we are happy to send you a PDF of the code from this volume.

It is even more awesome than it sounds… but in addition this will put you on our exclusive list of **Made Stupid Simple** fans and we will let you know about future titles in the **Made Stupid Simple** Series.

Get your free copy at:

## http://sixfigureteen.com/LuaBook

# LUA Scripting Made Stupid Simple

## *About This Manual*

This manual gives you a step-by-step programming lessons in Lua. This tutorial is designed for all those who are looking for a starting point to learn Lua.

The topics are suitable for both beginners as well as advanced users. This guide assumes that you know how to use a simple text editor and a command line interface.

## *Lua Programming*

Lua is an open source, powerful, fast, lightweight, and embeddable scripting language built on top of C programming language. It combines **simple syntax** with data description constructs based on arrays and semantics.

Lua is **dynamically typed**, and runs by interpreting bytecode for a register-based virtual machine. Its automatic memory management capability with incremental garbage collection, makes it **ideal for configuration, scripting, and rapid prototyping**.

## Install Lua

Before you can start programming in Lua, you need to install the program. **Two ways** you can do that:

- Either install the binary files at:
  _http://Lua-users.org/wiki/LuaBinaries_, or

- If you are using **Windows**, go to:
  _http://code.google.com/p/luaforwindows/_

  o For instructions on **Windows, Linux and Mac** instructions go here:
  http://www.tutorialspoint.com/lua/lua_envir onment.htm

Either way, you get everything exactly the same, no matter what operating system you are on. Just follow the on-screen instructions to install Lua.

My preference is to use the SciTE IDE so that I don't need to mess with the command prompt too much. In this manual we jump around a little bit so parts will look familiar and others won't depending on which OS and what Editor you are using.

The code will be the same regardless. If you don't want to install anything, or if you have trouble installing Lua with the instructions from the links above you could simple type the code into the online interpreter and Lua Terminal:

**Compile and Execute Online:**
Go to:
http://www.tutorialspoint.com/lua/lua_environment.htm

and look for the purple "Try it" button as pictured below:

Try the following example using our online compiler available at CodingGround ⧉

```
#!/usr/local/bin/lua

print("Hello World!")
```
⧉ Try it

## Online Terminal:
http://www.tutorialspoint.com/lua_terminal_online.php

### *Let's Start Writing Some Code*

The best way to learn a programming language is to start doing it.

```
▶ Execute    main.lua
1
2  print("Hello World!")
```

☑ Result

**Executing the program....**
**$lua main.lua**

Hello World!

As you can see above I've executed my "Hello World" using the online tool mentioned earlier but you can enter the code in your Lua IDE (like SciTE) and then click execute (which is usually a button that looks like the "Play" sign).

Alternately, you can save your code as a file and then execute it from the Lua Terminal. In that case, you are going to have the extension of Lua for all of your files such as, Luatut.Lua. It's that simple.

As pictured above, let's start with a "Hello World" message.

```
print ("Hello World")
```

If you are trying to execute the code from the file you will need to save your file and then jump over to your terminal and type:
`$lua luatut.lua`, and press Enter. "Hello World" is now showing on terminal.

## Commenting in Lua

You can make comments by typing 2 dashes on your text editor sublime:

-- Write your **single** line comments here.

--[[ Start your **multiline** comments here

and end with double brackets as well.

]]

## Variables and Data Types

Your variable names cannot start with a number, but they can contain numbers, letters, and underscores.
You can create one like this:

```
name = "Jordan" --This is a string variable.
```

Lua is dynamically typed based off of the data stored there, so this automatically becomes a string, because "Jordan" is a string. Your strings can either be double quotes (" ") or single quotes (' ') . It doesn't matter within Lua like it does in other languages *(just make sure they match – don't open with a double quote and end with a single quote).*

Another way for you to be able to print stuff out in Lua is like this:

```
name = "Jordan"
io.write("Size of string ", #name,
'\n')
```

As you can see, you can separate it if you want to put the string inside of the parenthesis. And on top of that, if you want to get the size and number of characters on your string, just put a # sign and name in this situation.

Then there are a bunch of things you can use backslash (\) for as a prefix. For example, '\n' is an easy way to skip to a new line.

**PLEASE NOTE:** that when you have multiple lines of code you should have a free line in between to make the separation clear – this isn't needed if the next line is supposed to be connected to the previous line like in IF statements or within FOR LOOPS).

**Backslashes**

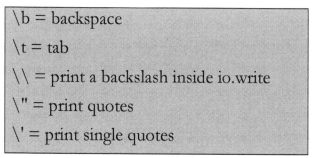

\b = backspace

\t = tab

\\ = print a backslash inside io.write

\" = print quotes

\' = print single quotes

You are also going to need a way to print a backslash inside something like io.write.

Backslash Quotes (\") are going to be used in situations where you have double quotes, but you want to put additional quotes inside of them. Like this:

**io.write** ("size \" of string")

You need to do this otherwise, it will not know where the string ended.

```
name = Jordan

io.write ("size of string", #name, '\n')
```

If you do File →Save the above and execute it, you will see "size of string" is 6 automatically printed out for you.

An interesting thing here is though this:

`name = 'Jordan'` is defined as a string correctly. You can define the name as 4.

```
name = 4
io.write ("size of string", #name,
'\n')
```

That is not an error. You can start as a string, and then convert the data, or the variable over into an integer (without having to explicitly call out the conversion).

```
name = 4
io.write("My name is ", name, "\n")
```

If you execute the above code, "my name is 4" is printed. No errors are thrown. However, other programming languages would throw errors if you try to do this because the data types would not match and most programming languages do not know what to do in that scenario other than to throw an error.

Lua only has "floating point" numbers, or what they call just "simple" numbers.

```
-- Lua only has floating point numbers and this is the max number
bigNum = 9223372036854775807 + 1
io.write("Big Number ", bigNum, "\n")

io.write("Big Number ", type(bigNum), "\n")

-- Floats are precise up to 13 digits
floatPrecision = 1.999999999999 + 0.0000000000005
io.write(floatPrecision, "\n")

-- We can create long strings and maintain white space
longString = [[
I am a very very long
string that goes on for
ever]]
io.write(longString, "\n")

-- Combine Strings with ..
longString = longString .. name
io.write(longString, "\n")

-- Booleans store with true or false
isAbleToDrive = true
io.write(type(isAbleToDrive), "\n")

-- Every variable gets the value of nil by default meaning it has no value
io.write(type(madeUpVar), "\n")
```

The biggest integer that you can store inside of Lua is 9223372036854775807 like in the following:

```
bigNum = 9223372036854775807
```

If you add 1 to that line, it will return a negative number.

```
io.write ("Big Number", bigNum)
```

That is as big as it gets with integers. You can come in here, surround it with type, and call it a **function** type. Jump over to where your code results are, and we can see Big Number prints out there, as well as $.

```
io.write ("Big Number",
type(bigNum), "n")
```

Every number, integers or floating point numbers are all considered just numbers inside of Lua. As we all know, floating point numbers are not necessarily precise.

```
BigNum = 9223372036854775807 + 1
floatPrecision = 1.999999999999 +
0.0000000000005
io.write (floatPrecision)
```

Basically with a floating number, you are going to have your digits be precise up to 13 digits:

```
1.9999999999995
```

If however, you add on an additional digit there, and re-run it, you are going to see that it has lost its precision. Your floating point numbers are accurate up to 13 digits, which is normally more than enough.

Let's say that we wanted to make a String that is going to go over multiple lines and at the same time, keep any white space that you would put inside those multiple lines how would you accomplish that? The answer is by using "[[ ]]" notation. The following line shows using this notation to open up a multiline string:

```
longString = [[
```

Inside those opening brackets (meaning after the opening two brackets shown above), type in:

```
I am a very  long
string that goes on
forever
]]
io.write(longString)
```

If you run this, it is going to not only print out the entire string, but also pay attention to any white space or new line that occurs within that long string. Try it for yourself.

For concatenation (combining strings) you will need to use a double period (..) in between two strings. If you want to combine strings inside of Lua, type:

```
longString = longString .. name
```

Like other programs, Lua also has Boolean data types.

```
isAbleToDrive = true
```

Let's say you wanted to monitor that a Boolean is going to either allow us to use a value of 'true' or 'false'. If we type the code below, it comes back as Boolean.

```
io.write(type(isAbleToDrive), '\n')
```

**Note**: Another little thing that is odd about Lua is that it does not go out of its way to show you the errors.

Now let's try a made-up variable:

```
io.write (type(madeUpVar), '\n')
```

Here, **madeUpVariable** has been made, created right there in that line, but hasn't been defined with any value yet. If you try to execute that, by default, Lua will return a value of 'nil'.

Well, this gives you a run down on what you need to know about variables in Lua. Now let's take a look at some/math functions.

## Math functions

In Lua, basic math functions are: add, subtract, divide, and multiply, just like in regular mathematics. Below are some basic functions that you can do in Lua:

```lua
io.write("5 + 3 = ",5+3,'\n')
io.write("5 - 3 = ",5-3,'\n')
io.write("5 * 3 = ",5*3,'\n')
io.write("5 / 3 = ",5/3,'\n')
io.write("5.2 % 3 = ",5%3,'\n')
```

This last line is the **modulus** %. Let's go ahead, save and execute it, and you are going to see exactly the results we are able to produce here.

Just pay attention that this is a **modulus** operation right here and not what is commonly known as a **remainder** operation. If it were a remainder operator, it would actually give the value of 2.2

Instead we see 5.2 % 3 = 2. and this is the modulus of a division by 3, so what it does is it automatically cuts that off.

Everything else here is pretty straight forward in regards to this basic mathematical operations. It is also important to know that you **cannot** perform common shorthand notations. For instance, the following are **NOT** valid within Lua:

```
Number ++
Number -
++ number
-- number
```

These are common in other languages, but the current version (v5.3) of Lua doesn't support it.

Another thing you **cannot do** is this type of shorthand notation:

Number += 1, which is normally equivalent to:

Number = Number + 1

If you want that, you just have to type it out (Number = Number +1).

```lua
io.write("floor(2.345) : ", math.floor(2.345), "\n")
io.write("ceil(2.345) : ", math.ceil(2.345), "\n")
io.write("max(2, 3) : ", math.max(2, 3), "\n")
io.write("min(2, 3) : ", math.min(2, 3), "\n")
io.write("pow(8, 2) : ", math.pow(8, 2), "\n")
io.write("sqrt(64) : ", math.sqrt(64), "\n")

-- Generate random number between 0 and 1
io.write("math.random() : ", math.random(), "\n")

-- Generate random number between 1 and 10
io.write("math.random(10) : ", math.random(10), "\n")

-- Generate random number between 1 and 100
io.write("math.random(1,100) : ", math.random(1,100), "\n")

-- Used to set a seed value for random
math.randomseed(os.time())

-- Print float to 10 decimals
print(string.format("Pi = %.10f", math.pi))
```

LUA has many built-in math operators: floor, ceil, max, min, sin, cos, tan, asin, acos, exp, log, log10, sprt, random, and randomseed (as seen in the above screenshot).

And I'll show you some examples of how all these work. We are going to check the flouring, the ceiling, the max, minimum and square root.

The only difference between floor and ceiling, is that the floor rounds the number down and the ceiling basically rounds it up. Max is going to give you the maximum; min is for minimum. And there are power and square root functions as well.

Random numbers are interesting, and you will probably use random numbers a lot in your programs. Let's generate a random number.

```
io.write("math.random() : ",
math.random(), '\n')
```

This will give you a random number between 0 and 1. But that is a bit boring. You may also have noticed here there is no semi colons at the end. You can put some semicolons in, but they are not mandatory.

Let's go instead and create a random number between 1 and 10. Just type in 10.

```
io.write("math.random(): ",
math.random (10), '\n')
```

Then here, you can also define numbers in very specific ranges. Let's say you wanted to go with a random number between 5 and 100. If we execute those, they all work pretty simply.

The other useful thing is that we can set our seed value, which will help us calculate a random value.

This is how we do it:

```
Math.randomseed(os.time())
```

That is going to generate a nice random value. We can also come in here and print our float values in different ways.

```
print(string.format)
```

I am going to be bouncing around a lot to show you the different ways you can use these things. If we wanted to format a string, you type:

```
print(string.format("Pi = %10f", math.pi))
```

Let's say we wanted to get "pi" is equal to and then import a value our string. Let's say we wanted it to be 10 decimal places long, "f" for float. We can also get the value of "pi" by the math library.

You will get the value of pi to 10 digits already sorted out for you. Also be aware that this is only going to have a precision of 13 digits.

Anything over that, and it is going to start botching itself up. That is the way floating numbers work in almost every computer language.

# Conditionals

Now that we have the math functions are out of the way, let's take a look at conditional statements. We are going to have relational operators as well as logical operators. Relational operators are going to be greater than, less than or equal to, equal, or not equal to.

**Relational Operators**: >, <, >=, <=, ==, ~=

**Logical Operators**: "and", "or", "not"

I am going to demonstrate how all of these work. Let's say you have an age which is equal to 13, and let's take a look at "if statements", and how they work.

```
if age < 16 then
    io.write("You can go to school", '\n')
    local localVar = 10
end
```

Another thing to be aware of is any variable we define inside of our "if statements", "for statements" and so on, will be called "local variables".

That just means they are local to this "if statement", and the value that is set here cannot be outside of the "if statement." (More on that later).

If this "If statement" does not come back as true, maybe we want to check something else. So we would go:

```
elseif (age >= 16) and (age<18) then
```

Then we can come in here and print something else out.

We can say something like:

```
elseif (age >= 16) and (age<18) then
   io.write("You can drive", '\n')
```

And then as a default we would use else, and throw something else in there.

```
else
   io.write("You can vote", '\n')
```

Whenever you have an "if statement", you always want to use "end" to finish it.

Let's jump back in here, and type:

print (localVar)

When we execute it, it will come back as "You can go to school", but this comes back as "nil". Like I said, once you define a local variable inside the "if statement", it cannot be accessed anywhere outside of the "if statement."

Let's play around with logical statements a little bit more to see how all of them work. See below:

```lua
age = 13

if age < 16 then
    io.write("You can go to school", "\n")
    local localVar = 10
elseif (age >= 16) and (age < 18) then
    io.write("You can drive", "\n")
else
    io.write("You can vote", "\n")
end
```

```lua
age = 13

if (age < 14) or (age > 67) then
    io.write("You    shouldn't    work\n")
    end
```

```lua
if (age < 14) or (age > 67) then io.write("You shouldn't work\n") end

-- Format, convert to string and place boolean value with string.format
print(string.format("not true = %s", tostring(not true)))

-- There is no ternary operator in Lua
-- canVote = age > 18 ? true : false

-- This is similar to the ternary operator
canVote = age > 18 and true or false
io.write("Can I Vote : ", tostring(canVote), "\n")

-- There is no Switch statement in Lua
```

Above "or" gives you a value of true and "then" operates with whatever is after the "then statement", if one or the other is true. "You shouldn't work" comes back if executed, because 13 is less than 14 *(of course I always loved child labor when I was a child laborer but that's not too popular to say these days).*

You can do this, but it gets sloppy, so watch out there. Just wanted to demonstrate how the logical operator works, to make you aware that you may see people use really sloppy long statements like that.

We can also format or convert multiple different variable types to other different variable types. We will also demonstrate the "not" logical operator as well. If you want to put a string inside of here, you just put a percent sign and an s (%s).

However, we are going to have to convert our **boolean** into a string, and convert our cast or conversion to string. You can put anything inside of here. Throw a number or anything else.

```
print(string.format("not true = %s",
tostring(not true)))
```

If you save that, you can see, "not true." This logical operator before the value of true is going to give us a value of false. You can also see how the Boolean value was converted to a string, so you can use it inside of our print statement.

There is no ternary operator in Lua. A ternary operator usually looks like:

```
canVote = age > 18 ? true : false
```

That is what a ternary operator usually looks like in other programming languages. It basically just says "if age is greater than 18, we want to assign the value of the word "true" to the value of "canVote"; otherwise we want to assign the value of "false" to the variable of canVote. We cannot do that. However, we can knock it off inside of Lua. Like this:

```
canvote = age > 18 and true or false
```

It looks very similar to the ternary operator and it works exactly like the ternary operator. We can say:

```
canvote = age > 18 and true or false

io.write("can i vote : ",
tostring(canvote))
```

You can see the answer comes back as false. This is an example of how you can use conditional statement, or "if else" and "else", as well as knock off a ternary operator.

It is also good to know that there is no "switch" function in Lua, but you can knock those off with "if" and "else" statements.

## Strings

Let's take a look at some strings and some ways we can work with them. I went and created a really long string right here for us to be able to play around with.

I am just going to do a couple of simple string operations that are common, and then as the tutorial continues, I will cover some more.

Let's say we wanted to get the quote length:

```
quote = "I changed my password to
incorrect. So that when I forget..."

io.write("Quote Length",
string.len(quote), '\n')
```

```
quote = "I changed my password everywhere to 'incorrect.' That way when I

io.write("Quote Length : ", string.len(quote), "\n")

-- Return the string after replacing
io.write("Replace I with me : ", string.gsub(quote, "I", "me"), "\n")

-- Find the index of a matching String
io.write("Index of password : ", string.find(quote, "password"), "\n")

-- Set characters to upper and lowercase
io.write("Quote Upper : ", string.upper(quote), "\n")
io.write("Quote Lower : ", string.lower(quote), "\n")
```

Make sure you separate everything with commas. You can see the quote length comes back at 111 characters.

We can come in here also and just throw the number sign inside, and get the same result.

**io.write**("Quote Length" , #quote, '\n')

This is the most common way to check the number of characters that you have in your string.

You can also come in here and replace certain strings. Let's say we wanted to replace "I" with "me." We can then go string.gsub, and then place the string you want to change, the value you want to change, and the value you are going to replace that with. Always make sure you close off all of your brackets.

**io.write**("Replace I with me... ", **string.gsub**(quote, "I", "me"), '\n')

If you File Save and execute, you are going to see that it changed all of the versions of "I" inside of this giant string with "me" instead.

Another thing we can do is to find any matching indexes. Everything inside of "n" with regards to strings is going to have an index for every character. The first letter is going to have an index of 0, the space is going to have an index of 1. The first "c" in the word "change" is going to have an index of 2, and so on.

We will be able to search within this long quote and find out what this index is. We are going to pass in the string we are going to be searching for, and then the word we are searching for.

In the situation below, we'll search for the word "password."

```
io.write("Index of password :
",string.find(quote, "password"),
'\n')
```

Save and execute, and the index of "password" is 14.

## Cases

If you wanted to make all of the characters inside of your quote uppercase, you can just put string.upper. Similarly, for lower case, use string.lower.

```
io.write("Quote Upper : ",
string.upper(quote), '\n')
io.write("Quote Lower : ",
string.lower(quote), '\n')
```

## Looping

Let's take a look at "Looping" and how that works inside of Lua.

We are going to start off with a While Loop. What we need to do is initialize our creative value that is going to define our starting value that we are going to be looping through.

While i<=10, we want to continue looping through or executing code inside of our WA loop.

```lua
i = 1
while (i <= 10) do
  io.write(i)
  i = i + 1

  -- break throws you out of a loop
  -- continue doesn't exist with Lua
  if i == 8 then break end
end
print("\n")

-- Repeat will cycle through the loop at least once
repeat
  io.write("Enter your guess : ")

  -- Gets input from the user
  guess = io.read()

  -- Either surround the number with quotes, or convert the string into
  -- a number
until tonumber(guess) == 15

-- Value to start with, value to stop at, increment each loop
for i = 1, 10, 1 do
  io.write(i)
end

print()
```

Let's step through some of the above pictured code:

```
i = 1
```

```
while (i <= 10) do
```

```
io.write(i)
```

```
i = i + 1
```

Again, you are not allowed to type something like i++. You have to type everything out.

Then let's say we would want to jump out of this loop, and not continue looping through it anymore.

```
if i == 8 then break end
end
```

You have to put an "end" to end the "if statement", but then you need another "end" to end our while loop (see picture). Then we will need a carriage return:

```
print('\n')
```

And then we can do something like print and throw a new line in there. If you execute that, it is going to print out the following:

**1234567**

It didn't continue printing up till 9 and 10 because we said that if it gets to the number 8 we want to jump outside of the loop and stop executing altogether.

It is important to understand that inside of LUA there is no continue statement.

```
--continue
```

You might be used to that in other computer languages, but it does not work here.

Another thing we can do, and this is more like the common "do while" loop in other programming languages, we have something else that is called the **"repeat"** statement.

We are going to say Repeat and continue to execute code

inside Lua as long as a condition is true.

Let's also demonstrate how you can get user input from the user. We can also store inside the variable 'guess', whatever they enter into the keyboard.

```
Repeat
    io.write ("Enter your guess : ")
    guess = io.read
```

That is how easy it is to get keyboard input. Then you are going to want to convert the "guess" they just made. It is automatically going to be stored as a string, but we want to convert it into a number.

If you want to convert to string you type in **tostring**, but we want to convert to a number, so type **tonumber**.

```
until tonumber(guess) == 15
```

This is going to be a little number guessing game in which it will continue asking them for a guess until they enter the number 15.

**$ lua luatut..lua** -- *or otherwise trigger the above code if you are not using a Lua terminal and saved file*

Enter your guess : 10
Enter your guess : 12
Enter your guess : 15

It is going to continue to ask until 15 is entered. That is how to use the Repeat Until or what is commonly known as the Do While in other languages.

Again, for Lua, it is known as Repeat Until.

## For Loops

Now let's take a look at For Loops. They are a little bit different. First we are going to define an iterator just like we did with the while loop previously. We are going to give it a starting value.

Then give it an ending value. Then we are going to say how much it should increment each time. We are going to throw in 1 and an "I" in there. You can also do a "break" statement as well, and see how that would work. It should cycle through and print 1 through 10.

```
for i = 1, 10, 1 do
   io.write (i)
 end
```

## Tables

This is a table, which is basically like an array in other programming languages. It will allow us to store multiple different values inside of it.

I jumped ahead to this right now to show you how easy it is to cycle through all of these different tables.

```
months = {"January", "February", "March",
"April", "June", "July", "August", "September",
"October", "November", "December"}
```

Key, then value, because everything in an A table will have a key, or an A value, or it is going to have an index by default, if you know how to assign a key.

```
for key, value in pairs (months) do
     io.write (value, " ")
end
```

We can then cycle through our table the way we cycled through indexes. In this situation, we want to print our values out to the screen.

Of course we have to end our open loop. Make sure you put value inside of the parenthesis (instead of v). If we execute it you are going to see that it prints out all of the different months with a space in between each one of those months.

We will also be able to do more interesting things with tables, but this is just a quick way to demonstrate all of those things.

Since we are on the subject of tables, let's take a look at how a table works. As I said, tables are going to take the place of arrays and dictionaries in other programming languages.

## Create a table

```
aTable = {}
```

```
-- Tables take the place of arrays, dictionaries, tuples, etc.

-- Create a Table
aTable = {}

-- Add values to a table
for i = 1, 10 do
  aTable[i] = i
end

-- Access value by index
io.write("First Item : ", aTable[1], "\n")

-- Items in Table
io.write("Number of Items : ", #aTable, "\n")

-- Insert in table, at index, item to insert
table.insert(aTable, 1, 0)
```

We can add values to the table using a for loop. You can add them on their own, but this is a quick way to add a whole bunch of values inside.

Everything is going to be stored inside of an index. This will increment through different values of **i**, as it assigns those values to **i**. The very first index in our table is going to have the value of 1. And of course, we are going to end that with an "end."

```
for i  =  1, 10 do
    aTable [i] = i
end
```

We can now access those using the index we have assigned. So let's say we want the very first value stored inside. You can probably guess exactly how we would find out the number of items we have inside of our table. We'll put a number sign inside the table. And this is how, we will be able to access those values.

```lua
io.write("First : ",  aTable[1], '\n')

io.write("Number of Items : ", #aTable, '\n')
```

The number of items is equal to 10, as you may have thought. We can also insert a value inside of a table. We are going to put "table."

Don't let this confuse you. aTable is the table and "table" is the liber we are going to use. If you want to insert a value, you write table.insert and the table we want to insert into.

We then define the index we want to insert into, and then the value we want to insert.

```lua
table.insert(aTable, 1, 0)

io.write("First : ", aTable [1], '\n')
```

If you print that out you will see the value of the first index inside of our table is 0. You could also change the value in aTable to 10.

```lua
io.write("First : ", aTable [10], '\n')
```

You can see when it is printed, everything is moved up as well, and it will come back as 9 instead of 10.

We can also take a table and convert it into a string, and then define how we want all of the items to be separated. In this case we will be using a comma (,)

```
print(table.concat(aTable, ", "))
```

You can see that when it prints out, the 0 is in there, because we inserted it there.

Another thing we can do with tables is, remove an item at a specific index. We would just type:

```
table.remove (aTable, 1)

print (table.concat(aTable, ", "))
```

When we print this, you can see it removed the 0 out of there.

We can also create Multi-Dimensional tables, and use a for loop to populate them. Then define an index you want to save inside of there.

That is also going to be a table, which we will populate by using the "for loop" again.

```
-- Combine a table as a String and seperate with provided seperator
print(table.concat(aTable, ", "))

-- Remove item at index
table.remove(aTable, 1)
print(table.concat(aTable, ", "))

-- Sort items in reverse
table.sort(aTable, function(a,b) return a>b end)
print(table.concat(aTable, ", "))

-- Create a multidimensional Table
aMultiTable = {}

for i = 0, 9 do
  aMultiTable[i] = {}
  for j = 0, 9 do
    aMultiTable[i][j] = tostring(i) .. tostring(j)
  end
end

-- Access value in cell
io.write("Table[0][0] : ", aMultiTable[1][2], "\n")

-- Cycle through and print a multidimensional Table
for i = 0, 9 do
  for j = 0, 9 do
    io.write(aMultiTable[i][j], " : ")
  end
  print()
end
```

You can also pull values from here and store them as strings. Then use "end" twice to close this for loop.

```
aMultiTable = {}
for i = 0, 9 do
 aMultiTable[i] = {}
 for j = 0, 9 do
   aMultiTable[i][j] = tostring(i) .. tostring(j)
 end
end
```

Now we can access the values that are stored inside the tables by using the indexes as well. We want to get whatever is being stored at the index of [0][0] inside of our multi-dimensional table. And you can see it comes back as 0.

```
io.write("Table[0][0] : ",
aMultiTable[0][0])
```

You can change the second set to 1 and 2 and it will come back as 12.

```
io.write("Table[0][0] : ",
aMultiTable[1][2])
```

That is how everything is stored inside the multi-dimensional table. We are going to use the exact same format for our for loop to cycle through and print out all of the items inside of our table.

```
for i = 0, 9 do
   for j = 0, 9 do
      io.write(aMultiTable[i][j], " : ")
   end
   print()
end
```

And you can see that every item is printed out there on our screen and exactly how they are formatted. You can play with it a little to get an idea of how tables are set up inside of Lua, and how to use them.

## Functions

Now let's take a look at "Functions". A function allows us to reuse our code, as well as better organize our code. We are going to create a function by typing in function and giving it a name.

If you want to pass values into a function to perform operations on them, you can do something like num1.

If you want to perform an operation and then send it back to whoever called for our function to operate, write return num1.

```
function getSum(num1, num2)
   return num1 + num2
end

print(string.format("5 + 2 = %d", getSum(5,2)))

function splitStr(theString)

   stringTable = {}
   local i = 1
```

For example:

```
function getSum(num1, num2)
   return num1 + num2
end
print(string.format("5 + 2 = %d",
getSum(5,2)))
```

Then you can see the answer and exactly how we are able to call that function. Let's come in and create another function. It is going to receive a string passed into it. Then we will create a stringTable.

We will be finding a local variable, and cycling through the string and store everything except for spaces inside of our table.

```
function splitStr(theString)

   stringTable = {}
   local i = 1
   for  str  in  string.gmatch(theString,
"[^%s] +") do
```

You are also capturing all of the strings up until the point there is a space with the carrot sign, percentage sign and s.

This is what is known as a "regular expression." Basically what this says is, we want to cycle through the string that they pass into our function, and we want to start capturing characters until we reach a space. That is what we are going to be storing inside of our stringTable.

We are cycling through the string. We are going to go stringTable, [i] for the index of the table. We are going to be pulling out each of those strings, and storing them temporarily in a variable named str, and then we are going to save them to our table. Then all we need is to increment our value for i, and end.

```
      stringTable [i] = str
      i = i + 1
   end
```

Now we are going to function return multiple values from a function. We would just return our stringTable, which is going to contain a bunch of values.

We are also going to send back the number of matches, the total number of words that we found inside of our string. Maybe this will make more sense if we replaced 'str' with 'word'.

```
for word in string.gmatch(theString, "[^%s]
+") do
    stringTable [i] = word
    i = i + 1
end
return stringTable, i
end
```

Either way it works or that is the way it operates. To end our function we type in "end." And then we will be able to return or receive those multiple values that were returned from this function called splitStr.

If we just do splitStrTable, this value in stringTable will be stored in splitStrTable. Then the number of strings inside of there will be the number of words. Then we just call our function.

```
splitStrTable, numOfStr =
splitStr("The Turtle")
```

```
-- Cycle through the String and store anything except for spaces
-- in the table
for str in string.gmatch(theString, "[^%s]+") do
  stringTable[i] = str
  i = i + 1
end

-- Return multiple values
return stringTable, i
end

-- Receive multiple values
splitStrTable, numOfStr = splitStr("The Turtle")

for j = 1, numOfStr do
  print(string.format("%d : %s", j, splitStrTable[j]))
end
```

We can then cycle through everything that was passed back inside the table. NumOfStr is the maximum amount we are going to loop through.

Then we can print on the screen, and format it. We can print our index separated by the individual words that were also passed back inside, and end our for loop.

```
for j = 1, numOfStr do
  print(string.format("%d : %s", j,
  splitStrTable[j]))
end
```

If you execute it, you will see "The Turtle", and then an extra "nil" from whenever we create tables. For me, doing this while using SciTE throws an error.

If we want, we can get rid of that by using (numOfStri – 1), and you will see it just prints out "The" and "Turtle."

```
for j = 1, (numOfStr-1) do
```

Your function, call and printing loop should look like the following:

```lua
function splitStr(theString)
    stringTable = {}
    local i = 1
    for word in string.gmatch(theString, "[^%s]+")
do
        stringTable [i] = word
        i = i + 1
    end
return stringTable, i
end

splitStrTable, numOfStr = splitStr ("The Turtle")

for j = 1, (numOfStr-1) do
    print(string.format("%d : %s", j, splitStrTable[j]))
end
```

That is how to go in and call a function, how to have it return multiple different values, how to split a string into a table, and how to return that value and save it into multiple different values, and cycle through it.

So there is a whole bunch of different ways we can use functions inside Lua.

## Variadic functions

Now let's talk about variadic functions. This is how we are going to be able to receive an unknown number of parameters inside our functions.

```lua
function getSumMore(...)
  local sum = 0

  for k, v in pairs{...} do
    sum = sum + v
  end
  return sum
end

io.write("Sum : ", getSumMore(1,2,3,4,5,6), "\n")
```

If we do not know how many different parameters or attributes that can be set inside the parenthesis, we can just put 3 little dots inside. In the above example, **k** is the key and **v** is the value.

**Pairs** Is going to be passed in as a table and the curly brackets {...} will make sure to keep cycling through, depending upon the number of attributes or parameters that were passed inside.

**NOTE**: if you are using an editor that converts three periods (.) into an single ellipsis character this will cause an error because LUA is looking for three separate periods for this notation.

```lua
function getSumMore(...)
  local sum = 0
  for k, v in pairs{...} do
     sum = sum + v
  end
  return sum
end

io.write("Sum", getSumMore(1,2,3,4,5,6), '\n')
```

The Sum should come back as 21. So that's how we are able to pass in an unknown number of parameters and then use it.

An interesting thing inside Lua is that a function is a variable, in that we can store them under variable names as well as we store tables. We can also pass and return them through functions. So let's demonstrate that.

```lua
doubleIt = function(x) return x * 2 end
print (doubleIt(4))
```

We have basically made "doubleIt" a function. It is also a variable. This should automatically pop out the number 8.

## Closure

Along those same lines, a closure is a function that can access local variables of an enclosing function. Let's create one. We call it outerFunc because this is going to be an outer function that will contain our closure.

We'll see why this is interesting. We will create a local variable, and put an inner function inside of it with return function, and then inside of this inner function let's increment the value of i.

```
function outerFunc()
 local i = 0
 return function()
          i = i + 1
          return i
       end
end
```

So this is a function inside of a closure. Whenever you include an inner function in a function, that inner function is going to remember any changes made to the variable inside the inner function.

Let's store our function inside a variable called getI.

```
getI = outerFunc()
print(getI())
print(getI())
```

The reason this is a closure because you are going to continue to increment and store the changing values of **i** that are inside.

If you run this the value of **i** starts out as 1, but then when it is run a second time, it will increment even though we've assigned the value of 0 to local **i**.

So that is an example of a closure, exactly how they work, and how they store values as they are being called multiple different times.

## Coroutines

Now let's look at something similar called a "Coroutine." A Coroutine is similar to a thread in other programming languages, except that they cannot run in parallel.

A Coroutine is either going to have a status of running suspended, dead, or normal. You will see what all of those look like.

```
co = coroutine.create(function()
    for i = 1, 10, 1 do
    print(i)
    print(coroutine.status(co))
    if i == 5 then coroutine.yield() end
    end end)

-- They start off with the status suspended
print(coroutine.status(co))
```

Let's create a coroutine.

By printing the coroutine.status, we can see the changing statuses from running suspended, dead, or normal. If we want to pause or yield over to another coroutine, we just type in coroutine yield.

```
co = coroutine.create(function()
    for i = 1, 10, 1 do
    print (i)
    Print(coroutine.status(co))
    if i == 5 then coroutine.yield()  end
  end
end)
```

```
print(coroutine.status(co))

co2 = coroutine.create(function()
  for i = 101, 110, 1 do
  print(i)
  end end)

coroutine.resume(co2)
coroutine.resume(co)
```

If we want to check our coroutine and see its status whenever it first starts, type:

**`print(coroutine.status(co))`**

This status starts off as suspended. Now we can call for this coroutine to resume or start executing, and then come in and also check the status after we tell it to start running.

**`coroutine.resume(co)`**
**`print (coroutine.status (co))`**

If you run this, you can see it starts off as suspended, and runs until it hits 5. That is because we want to yield this code routine and stop its execution by telling it when to stop.

We will now, create another coroutine that we are going to run at the same time, very much like we would do with threads in other programming languages.

```
co2 = coroutine.create(function()
for i = 101, 110, 1 do
    print (i)
end end)
```

If we do coroutine.resume, and then continue execution inside of our original coroutine that we created, we can see the process if you execute.

```
coroutine.resume(co2)
coroutine.resume(co)
```

It starts off as suspended, goes up to 5 running, then it gets suspended, jumps over to the other coroutine, which doesn't get suspended.

It goes through its entire process. Whenever we call the coroutine to continue execution, it continues executing until it is finally dead.

If we get the status of the coroutine from the line above:

```
print(coroutine.status(co))
```

It is in fact dead after it has done or executed all of the code inside of it.

## File I/O

Now let's take a look at something that a lot of people are confused about because there isn't a lot of information online about it; that is File I/O.

There are many different ways we can operate on files. See all the different ways right here:

| | |
|---|---|
| r: | Read only (default) |
| w: | Overwrite or create a new file |
| a: | Append or create a new file |
| r+ : | Read & Write existing file |
| | Overwrite read or create a file |
| w+: | Append read or create file |
| a+ : | |

If we want to create a new file that we are going to be working with, but also overwrite and read from that file, we'll do this:

```
file = io.open ("test.lua", "w+")
```

```
-- Create new file for reading and writing
file = io.open("test.lua", "w+")

-- Write text to the file
file:write("Random string of text\n")
file:write("Some more text\n")

-- Move back to the beginning of the file
file:seek("set", 0)

-- Read from the file
print(file:read("*a"))

-- Close the file
file:close()
```

You've just created a file and you will be able to overwrite it, and read from. If you want to create some text for the file, you'd just type:

**file:write("Random String of text \n")**

We can use add new lines inside the existing lines. Let's say we want to put some more stuff in our files, we'll just say write again.

**file:write("Some more text\n")**

We can use "seek" to move to the beginning of our file, set and then the index where we want to jump because everything is indexed inside of string, so we're going to jump to the beginning of our file.

**file:seek("set", 0)**

If we want to go and read everything from our file we could do the following:

**print(file:read("\*a"))**

So we wrote to our file, we created our file, we jumped back to the beginning of our file, and we are going to read everything from that point. The next thing we need to do is close our file.

**file:close()**

If you print this out, you will see "random string of text" and "some more text."

Now let's say we wanted to continue working with our file, but we wanted to append data to the end of our file. How do we do that?

We can leave this named as file because Lua is real nice about stuff like that. We are going to type in the name of the file we want to work with.

In this situation we want to append, so we will say a+. Then write some new information to our file.

```
file = io.open("test.lua", "a+")

file:write("Even more text\n")

file:seek("set", 0)

print(file:read("*a"))

file:close()
```

```
file = io.open("text.lua", "a+)
file.write("Even more text\n")
```

If you want to read from a file you have to jump back to the beginning of it, so we are going to use "seek" to do that. We are going to say set and exactly where we want to jump to.

You can put any index to jump around the file, but we are going to use 0 here. We are going to read data, and of course we want all of that data. Then finally we want to close our file.

```
file:seek("set", 0)
print(file:read("*a")
file:close()
```

If we do all of that, save it, and run it, we see "Random string of text", "Some more text" and "Even more text" printed on our screen. Now we are going to be able to work with our files inside of Lua.

## Modules

Basically a module is like a library that is full of functions and variables. We are going to create a module, and then use it inside of our programs. Let's create a module.

### File→Save using the name Convert.lua

It is important that your File name and Module name **are exactly the same**. To create one:

### local convert = {}

There is our module. Inside of this we can put a function, like convert feet centimeters.

This function is going to receive an attribute of feet, and it is going to return whatever that value is, times 30.48. Then end, return the module and save it.

```
function convert.ftToCm
    return  feet + 30.48
end
return convert
```

Just make sure you have convert in those 3 places, and that the name of the file is convert. Now we can work with this module function.

If you want to be able to get access that they have to be in the same directory. Here, we'll want 3 decimal places with a floating point number, and we're going to call our module, and pass in a value of 12.

```
-- ------------ MODULES -----------
-- A Module is like a library full of functions and variables

-- Use require to gain access to the functions in the module
convertModule = require("convert")

-- Execute the function in the module
print(string.format("%.3f cm", convertModule.ftToCm(12)))
```

```lua
convertModule = require("convert")

print(string.format("%.3f cm",
convertModule.ftToCm(12)))
```

You will see, it returns the answer of 42.480 cm. So that's a quick example of how we can work with modules in Lua.

## Metatable

A metatable lets us define how operations on tables should be carried out in regards to adding tables together, subtracting, multiplying, dividing, concatenating, comparing tables, and so on.

Let's come in and create a table and put some default values in it, using a for loop to fill it up with stuff.

```
aTable  =  {}
for x = 1, 10  do
    aTable[x]  =  x
end
```

So there we have a table. Now we are going to define our Metatable. We are going to define how table values should be added.

We will see how the tables should be added, how they should be subtracted and multiplied, how they should be divided, and how they should be combined, and so on.

In this scenario, we are going to pass in 2 tables and define how those 2 tables are going to be added together, by creating a sumTable, which is going to be the table that will be returned.

```
mt = {
__add =  function(table1, table2)
    sumTable  =  {}
```

We also want to check and make sure that the table values are not equal to nil, which has to be true for both tables.

```
for y = 1, #table1 do
   if {table1[y] ~= nil) and (table2[y] ~= nil) then
```

Then we will start adding stuff to the sumTable. You can decide how you want to add table values. We are going to take the values of table 1 and 2 and store them inside a brand new table.

If one of the tables comes back as nil, we are going to say that we want to store 0 inside of there. We make up the rules in this situation. We want to close off our "if statement" and our "for statement."

```
sumTable[y] = table1[y]  +  table2[y]
else
   subTable[y] = 0
   end
 end
return sumTable
end,
```

Then after we have created our brand new table, with all of the sums inside of it, we want to return it and end it.

I can also check how table values are going to be checked for equality. The way we do that is:

```
__eq = function(table1, table2)
   return table1.value == table2.value
   end,
}
```

If both of those come back, then we know that is going to work for us.

Another thing we can do is we can also check if it is less than. I'm going to let this be your homework assignment.

Figure out how to make sure these values work for whether a table is less than, or if it is less than or equal to (<=).

```
-- Define how table values should be checked for equality
__eq = function (table1, table2)
  return table1.value == table2.value
end,

-- For homework figure out how to check if less then
__lt = function (table1, table2)
  return table1.value < table2.value
end,

-- For homework figure out how to check if less then or equal
__le = function (table1, table2)
  return table1.value <= table2.value
end,
}
}
```

Also to figure out how subtraction, multiplication and division work. **Hint**: it is going to be something very similar to what we've worked with above.

--CHECK IF THIS IS LESS THAN
```
    __lt = function (table1, table2)
      return table1.value < table2.value
```

--CHECK IF THIS IS LESS THAN OR EQUAL TO
```
    __le = function (table1, table2)
      return table.value <= table2.value
      end,
```

}

Now that we have our Metatable all set up, we need to attach the Meta Methods to our table. How do you do that? First set Metatable, and provide the table you are going to assign it to. And then you can come in and check if they were equal.

```
setmetatable(aTable, mt)
print(aTable == aTable)
```

If you do that and execute it, you will see that it comes back as true. Now we are going to test what we did in regards to adding tables. Let's create a new table called addTable.

We then create a simple for loop that allows us to cycle through our new addTable we've just created. When we execute it, it is going to add all of those values together in our brand new table and print them out on the screen.

```
-- Attach the metamethods to this table
setmetatable(aTable, mt)

-- Check if tables are equal
print(aTable == aTable)

addTable = {}

-- Add values in tables
addTable = aTable + aTable

-- print the results of the addition
for z = 1, #addTable do
  print(addTable[z])
end
```

```
addTable = {}

addTable = aTable + aTable

for z = 1, #addTable do
    print(addTable[z])
end
```

So that is Metatables and Meta Methods, and how we can work with them.


## Object-oriented programming

Now let's take a look at Object-Oriented Programming (OOP), or at least Lua's version of OOP.

So that we're clear on this, Lua is not an OOP language, and it does not allow you to define classes. But you can in some ways fake it by using tables and metatables.

What we are going to do is, create an Animal table. Then create all of the default values for everything inside of it. We will define animal's height, weight, name and an animal sound.

```
-- Define the defaults for our table
Animal = {height = 0, weight = 0, name = "No Name", sound = "No Sound"}

-- Used to initialize Animal objects
function Animal:new (height, weight, name, sound)

  setmetatable({}, Animal)

    -- Self is a reference to values for this Animal
  self.height = height
  self.weight = weight
  self.name = name
  self.sound = sound

  return self
end
```

## Animal = {height = 0, weight = 0, name = "No Name", sound = "No Sound"}

There is the table we have created for Animal, or the object we are trying to create inside of here. Now we have to define a function for our table that is going to allow us to initialize this.

## function Animal:new(height, weight, name, sound)

Very similar to an Object oriented programming language. Then we have to set our metatable, throwing in a junk table.

## setmetatable({}, Animal)

That is how easy it is to create that metatable. Now if we want to refer to height, weight, name and sound for our animal objects, we use self, because we do not know what the name of it is.

**self.height = height**

We want to do that for all of the other attributes we want for our animal objects.

**self.weight = weight**
**self.name = name**
**self.sound = sound**

We are creating it in very similar ways what you have seen in other programming languages. This is going to initialize and create a new animal object, and after it initializes everything, it will return that animal object. Of course, end the function with "end", as usual.

```
        return  self
end
```

Let's say we wanted to also create a function that is going to allow us to print out information about our Animal object.

We will call it toString. It is not going to receive anything ().

```
function Animal:toString()
animalStr = string.format("%s weighs %.1f lbs, is %1f in tall and says %s", self.name, self.weight, self.height, self.sound)
  return animalStr
end
```

This is another way of using string format. The "selfs" allow us to import all of those things for our specific Animal into our toString function.

So we've created an object function, initialized it, used defaults and a metatable we defined for it. Pretty similar to things we have seen in the past.

Let's go and create an Animal Object. First, we are going to call it Spot. We are going to call our initialization function, then pass some junk values inside.

```lua
-- Outputs a string that describes the Animal
function Animal:toString()

  animalStr = string.format("%s weighs %.1f lbs, is %.1f in tall and says %s

  return animalStr
end
-- Create an Animal
spot = Animal:new(10, 15, "Spot", "Roof")

-- Get variable values
print(spot.weight)

-- Call a function in Animal
print(spot:toString())
```

```lua
spot = Animal:new(10, 15, "Spot", "Woof")
```

We just called for our animal object to be initialized. We could then print Spot's weight and call the function.

```lua
print(spot.weight)
print(spot:toString())
```

It doesn't have to have the name **toString**. That is just the name we gave it. And if you run that, you should see that it works. 15 comes out, because that is how we are accessing the weight, with the dot operator.

Then we can call that function, which is automatically going to get all of that information about Spot, and print it on our screen.

## Inheritance

You may ask yourself does "Inheritance" work in Lua. Yes it does, and we'll show you how to use it. Let's say we wanted to create a brand new object called Cat.

We can inherit all of the functions defined inside of our animal object just by calling new.

```
Cat = Animal:new()

function Cat:new (height, weight, name, sound, favFood)
    setmetatable({}, Cat)
```

## Cat = Animal:new()

Now we have all of the toString, the height, weight, name and sound inside of our new cat object. We can of course overwrite any of the functions. So one of the functions we might want to overwrite is "new" and how it works inside of our new cat object.

Well we are just going to replace Animal with cat. And let's say our cat objects are going to store favFood and not just height, weight, name and sound. We are going to set our metaTable to be Cat, instead of Animal. Then the only thing we need to change is favFood.

```
self.height = height
self.weight = weight
self.name = name
self.sound = sound
self.favFood = favFood

return self
end
```

```
function Cat:new(height, weight, name,
sound, favFood)
      setmetatable ({}, Cat)

      self.height  =  height
      self.weight  =  name
      self.name  =  name
      self.sound  =  sound
      self.favFood  =  favFood

    return self
end
```

After return, everything is going to work exactly the same. We can then also come in and overwrite our **toString** function.

Remember, we just changed Animal new to Cat new. We are going to do the same for **toString**. We are going to add what kind of food it loves.

**function** Cat : **toString**()

**catStr** = string.format("%s weighs %.1f lbs, is %.1f in tall and says %s and loves %s", self.name, self.weight, self.height, self.sound, self.favFood)

**return** catStr
**end**

Now let's create a Cat.

```
function Cat:toString()

  catStr = string.format("%s weighs %.1f lbs, is %.1f in tall, says %s and

  return catStr
end
-- Create a Cat
fluffy = Cat:new(10, 15, "Fluffy", "Meow", "Tuna")

print(fluffy:toString())
```

fluffy = Cat:**new**(10, 15, "Fluffy", "Meow", "Tuna")
**print**(fluffy:toString())

When you run it you can see that Fluffy weighs 15 lbs., is 10-inch tall, says Meow, and loves Tuna.

There you go guys. There is a ton of information about Lua but we hope that this has truly been...

# LUA Scripting
# Made Stupid Simple!

# FREE GIFT – Lua Code in COLOR

## The Code Used in This Volume IN COLOR

Courtesy of our friend Derek Banas (from *New Think Tank*) we are happy to send you a PDF of the code from this volume (only with Derek's name since he inspired this volume).

It is even more awesome than it sounds… but in addition this will put you on our exclusive list of **Made Stupid Simple** fans and we will let you know about future titles in the **Made Stupid Simple** Series.

Get your free copy at:

## http://sixfigureteen.com/LuaBook

Jordan Kaufman

# ABOUT THE AUTHOR

**Jordan Robert Kaufman** has almost two decades of experience in technology centered primarily around enterprise software, audio engineering, and alternative animation techniques.

Kaufman also recently started an online community called www.SixFigureTeen.com which promotes youth entrepreneurship, education and alternatives to college.

He resides in the American Southwest with his amazingly supportive wife and family.

jordanrkaufman@gmail.com
**Twitter**: @Jordan_RK

50782826R00044

Made in the USA
Lexington, KY
30 March 2016